"A vision without action is just a dream. Action without a vision is merely a passing of time. But a vision with action can change the world!"

Dedication

I dedicate this book

to my wife Syreeta and our newborn baby Jade.

I thank God

for planting this vision in my heart.

First Edition 2007
Printed in the United States of America.
ISBN: 978-0-9791104-0-5

Published by Success By Choice, Inc.
11700 Monticello Avenue
Silver Spring, MD 20902

www.successbychoice.com
purpose@successbychoice.com

Congratulations!

I congratulate you for participating in this 40-day *LIVING WITH PURPOSE* program. Your commitment to experiencing the most out of your life is exciting! For you to begin this transformational program at this time in your life illustrates that you are now ready to take your life to the next level with new results.

Is it going to be easy? No, but it can be done. All it requires is believing that it's possible for you to live your *ideal* life and taking action as though you believe.

This *LIVING WITH PURPOSE* program is designed to make you think more deliberately about your life. No more sleep-walking! No more being unconscious to the choices that you are making. What you do today will dictate where you will be tomorrow.

This 40-day program will inspire you to maximize your true potential. Remember, if you are "casual" about your life, your dreams will ultimately become a "casualty." You will die with your true dreams and potential still in you.

To get the most from this *LIVING WITH PURPOSE* program, you must work and complete the questions, exercises, and action items. No more excuses! No more "Would of...Should of...Could of...BUT Didn't!" No more procrastination!

Our team is committed to supporting your breakthroughs and growth. Feel free to email your insights to purpose@successbychoice.com so that we may celebrate your victories with you.

Get ready because your life will never be the same. You will be inspired to make the most of your life.

Let's now begin!

Your Success Is Your Choice!

Marlon

"The greatest tragedy is not death, but life without purpose. Without a clear purpose, you have no foundation on which you base decisions, allocate your time, and use your resources. You will tend to make choices based on circumstances, pressures, and your mood at that time."

- Rick Warren

Contents

DAY 1

Uncovering the Greatness Within You!

There is greatness within you!

That's right! I'm talking about you. Do you believe me?

Say it aloud, "There is greatness within me!" One more time..."There is greatness within me!"

How do you feel when you say it?...Do you believe it?...Is it really true?

Let me get straight to the point! It is absolutely true.

There is GREATNESS within YOU!

Why do I say this?

It's because you have so much potential. Whether you believe it or not...it's TRUE!

There are no mistakes. You are reading this page at this exact moment in your life because it's time to maximize your true potential. Now is the time to take your life to the next level. Because when you are committed, you will produce *new* results.

You may be thinking, "Who are you to tell me there's greatness within me? You don't even know me."

Yes, that may be true. However, I know the truth about you—you were born on purpose.

Think about it! For you to get to where you are in your life right now, you had to overcome various challenges, deal with personal insecurities, and even move away from some negativity.

Sure, life has not always been easy—but you're still standing. And that's why I say, "There is greatness within you." In spite of all you've encountered and experienced, you are still here.

Is life fair? No, absolutely not! But the beautiful thing about life is that once we truly reflect upon our experiences, we come to see our challenges from another perspective.

There is power when we realize that our "challenges" are really "blessings" in disguise because they allow us to GROW stronger.

So what are some character-building moments that you have experienced? Take time to remember your feelings, your excitement, lessons learned, and your breakthroughs.

Think about some important decisions and experiences that you have had.

Some may be major challenges while others may be times when you were totally happy. Remember how each defining moment has contributed to your life. Write your five defining moments on the next page.

Five Defining Moments of My Life:

1. _____
2. _____
3. _____
4. _____
5. _____

Life is a full range of emotions where sometimes we're happy, and at other times we're sad. It's like our feelings are on an emotional roller coaster where we go up and down and then up again.

Review your list of "Five Defining Moments." Take time to reflect upon your defining moments. How did these experiences contribute to your growth? What did you learn as a result of these particular experiences? Write your insights here:

_____
_____
_____
_____
_____
_____

Do you now see more value in these experiences? As you make time to reflect upon your daily experiences, you begin appreciating life more. Now let me ask you, "Are you happy?"

Some people think, "When I get that promotion, then I'll be totally happy." Or "When I find Mr. Right or Miss Beautiful, then I'll be totally happy." Or "When I buy my dream home and dream car, then I'll be totally happy."

But this is a façade because true success and happiness is not a destination. True success and happiness is a journey. That's right! A journey! And I'm here to say, "Your life matters." Everything that you've experienced so far in your life has gotten you to this exact point. Both the "good" and the "bad" have contributed to who you are today.

Remember this:

It's not what happens to you that matters. Rather, it's how you choose to respond to life experiences that determines who you REALLY are.

The reason some people are not living up to their true potential is because they are so caught up in the "BUSY-ness" of life: going to school, work, another meeting, and then rushing to that next commitment...And when they finally reach home, there are more activities to complete. This routine continues and continues where they wake up the next morning, go to school/work, go to meetings, complete assignments, go shopping, go home, cook dinner, talk on the phone, watch TV, go to sleep...and then wake up and go to school/work, go to meetings, complete assignments, go shopping, go home, cook dinner, talk on the phone, watch TV, go to sleep... You get the point.

And so with a life like this, when do you stop and give yourself the gift of quiet time for personal reflection? Making reflection time a priority will definitely enhance your life.

"How do you have a successful life?" I would venture to say, "Many successful years!" Because the years add up to contribute to one's total life.

So how do you have a successful year? Yes, you know the answer: "Many successful months!" And how do you have a successful month? You now know where I'm going. Of course, "Many successful weeks."

Let's ask the final question: "How do you have a successful week?" Exactly, "Many successful days." So you can infer that the quality of your life comes down to what you do with the specific moments of each day.

Time is our most precious commodity. Yet, for many people, the hours of a day seem to pick up speed, turning months into faint memories as the weeks pass by so quickly. **How do you slow down the clock to truly enjoy your journey through life?**

One suggestion is to take time from the busy-ness of each day to slow down and reflect upon your daily joys, character-building experiences, life-altering situations, and precious moments. From this day forward, make the commitment to:

Write everyday in your Gratitude Success Journal ...

where you answer one of the following questions:

- What was great about today?
- What did I learn today?
- What made me smile or laugh today?
- What am I grateful for in my life right now?
- What did I do today to move closer to fulfilling my true life mission?
- Who loves me and whom do I love?
- What did I do today to demonstrate my leadership skills?
- What am I most proud of in my life right now?
- What did I do today to contribute to someone else?
- How did I grow today?

Journaling is critically important for your personal and professional success. By reflecting upon your daily experiences, you will begin learning new life lessons that ultimately contribute to your growth.

Throughout this *LIVING WITH PURPOSE* program, you will answer specific questions that will empower you.

Questions like, *"What is your life really about?"*

When you're 95 years old, what's going to matter the most to you?

For me, it will be two things:
      1) the loving relationships in my life and
      2) the defining moments that I have experienced.

So when you're 95 years old, what will be important to you?

Answering thought-provoking questions is critically important to being your best because questions make you think. Your mind is a computer —for every question you ask of yourself, you will get an answer.

So one way to experience more out of life is by asking

and answering...

Assignment

Today's assignment is to answer four specific questions. Take your time and really think about your answers. This assignment is for you. You do not have to share your answers with anyone, so give yourself the gift of being truthful. You will be amazed at what you learn about yourself by answering these questions with complete honesty.

 What are your five, most important, life-defining moments? Be Specific.

1. _____

2. _____

3. _____

4. _____

5. _____

Assignment

 Why do these experiences mean so much to you?

1. _____
_____
_____
_____
_____

2. _____
_____
_____
_____

3. _____
_____
_____
_____
_____

4. _____
_____
_____
_____

5. _____
_____
_____
_____

Assignment

 What have you learned from these five character-building situations?

1. _____
_____
_____
_____
_____

2. _____
_____
_____
_____

3. _____
_____
_____
_____
_____

4. _____
_____
_____
_____

5. _____
_____
_____
_____
_____

Assignment

 How have you grown and become a stronger person as a result of these life-defining moments?

1. _____
_____
_____
_____
_____

2. _____
_____
_____
_____

3. _____
_____
_____
_____
_____

4. _____
_____
_____
_____
_____

5. _____
_____
_____
_____
_____

"Each of us must earn our own existence. And how does anyone earn anything? Through perseverance, hard work and desire."

- Thurgood Marshall

DAY 2

Empowering Questions

What are you most proud of in your life right now?

_____
_____
_____
_____
_____
_____
_____
_____
_____
_____
_____
_____
_____
_____
_____
_____
_____
_____
_____
_____
_____
_____
_____

"We realize that your future lies chiefly in your own hands. In order to succeed, you must practice the virtues of self-reliance, self-respect, industry, perseverance and economy."

- Paul Robeson

DAY 3

Empowering Questions

What was good about today?

_____
_____
_____
_____
_____
_____
_____
_____
_____
_____
_____
_____
_____
_____
_____
_____
_____
_____
_____
_____
_____
_____

"Success is finding your purpose, developing it to its full potential and sowing seeds for others."

- John Maxwell

DAY 4

Empowering Questions

What are you grateful for in your life right now?

_____
_____
_____
_____
_____
_____
_____
_____
_____
_____
_____
_____
_____
_____
_____
_____
_____
_____
_____
_____
_____

"I'm not a self-made man. I cannot forget those who have sacrificed for me to get where I am today."

- Jessie Hill

DAY 5

Empowering Questions

What did you learn today that makes you a better person?

_____
_____
_____
_____
_____
_____
_____
_____
_____
_____
_____
_____
_____
_____
_____
_____
_____
_____
_____
_____
_____
_____

"It's not what you take but what you

leave behind that defines greatness."

- Edward Gardner

DAY 6

Empowering Questions

What did you do today to contribute to someone else?

_____
_____
_____
_____
_____
_____
_____
_____
_____
_____
_____
_____
_____
_____
_____
_____
_____
_____
_____
_____
_____
_____
_____
_____
_____
_____

"The only justification for ever looking down on somebody is to pick them up."

- Jesse Jackson

DAY 7

Empowering Questions

What did you do today to move closer to fulfilling your true purpose?

_____
_____
_____
_____
_____
_____
_____
_____
_____
_____
_____
_____
_____
_____
_____
_____
_____
_____
_____
_____
_____
_____
_____

"If a man is called to be a street sweeper, he should sweep streets even as Michaelangelo painted, or as Beethoven composed music, or as Shakespeare wrote poetry. He should sweep streets so well that all the hosts of heaven and earth will pause to say, 'Here lived a great street sweeper who did his job well.'"

- Martin Luther King

Moving Through FEar

Have you been taking action to make your dreams come true?

Be honest.

Have you really done your best in making things happen?

Are you not taking action because of fear?...fear of rejection?...fear of failing?...fear of being embarrassed?...fear of...

Well, let me ask you, **"Is FEar real?"**

Yes or No? Circle your answer.

Now go ahead and write your reasons for your answer.

_____

_____

_____

_____

_____

_____

_____

_____

_____

_____

Let's get something straight, right here and right now. *If you do not step outside your comfort zone and face your fears, you will never fulfill your true potential.*

This is the truth.

Empowering Questions

When you reflect upon your life, do you have any regrets? If so, what are some of them?

_____
_____
_____
_____
_____

Review your list of regrets. Why didn't you take action? Was it because of fear? Be specific and detailed in your answers.

_____
_____
_____
_____
_____

How has FEAR stopped you from being your best?

_____
_____
_____
_____
_____

Describe a time when you allowed FEAR to stop you from taking action.

_____

_____

_____

_____

_____

_____

_____

_____

_____

_____

What have you learned from this experience?

_____

_____

_____

_____

_____

_____

_____

_____

_____

_____

What are some missed opportunities because you did not take action?

_____

_____

_____

_____

_____

_____

_____

_____

_____

FEAR holds a lot of people back from being their best! And because they didn't take action and face their fears, they now have regrets.

Regardless of what has happened in the past, it's gone. Don't get stuck in the past. Today is a new day, so get excited. By making new choices, your life will take on new meaning.

When **FEAR** comes up, you have a choice:

Do you allow **FEAR** to stop you **OR** do you move through FEAR by taking action?

Unfortunately, many people allow **FEAR** to stop them and they turn around, never fulfilling their true potential.

F.E.A.R.
False Expectations Appearing Real

Now if **FEAR** is false expectations, then why do so many people allow **FEAR** to hold them back from taking action?

It's because some people blow things out of perspective, making the consequences worse than they really are.

Having the proper perspective will empower you to move through fear. Whenever you want to do something but you're scared, ask yourself these two empowering questions:

1. What's the worst thing that can happen if I take action?

2. If I don't take action, what will it cost me?

These two questions have encouraged many people to take action in spite of their fears.

Whenever I'm standing in front of **FEAR**, scared to do something,

> I ask myself **Question #1:**
> *"What's the worst thing that can happen if I take action?"*

Just by answering this question, I now put my fears into their proper place.

My perspective is: As long as I'm not going to die, then I'll take action. Remember, a coward dies a thousand deaths but a leader with courage is victorious!

> Next, I ask myself **Question #2:**
> *"If I don't take action, what will it cost me?"*

I realize that if I don't take action, I will have regrets. And that's definitely not the way to live life.

You and I have so much potential. I believe a major regret is when a person reflects back upon his or her life and realizes that there were so many opportunities that were never seized.

And why is this?

It's because this person did not step outside his or her comfort zone and take action. Instead, this person just played it safe and now has major regrets.

By answering these two questions on a continuous basis, your life will take on new meaning. You will face your fears by taking action. You will step outside your comfort zone, knowing that your life is to be experienced to the fullest.

Remember,
there is GREATNESS within you!

You must no longer allow FEAR to hold you back from living your true purpose.

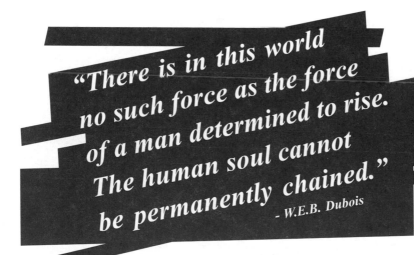

"There is in this world no such force as the force of a man determined to rise. The human soul cannot be permanently chained."
- W.E.B. Dubois

Assignment

 For the next three days, you will take action in spite of your initial fears. You will record your fears, the actions you took, and the corresponding results.

When you take action in spite of your fears, you are building your courage and belief in yourself.

By recording specific situations where you faced your fears and still took action, you will develop more confidence. This will transform your life because faith and fear cannot operate at the same time.

For me,
I choose to live by walking
with faith and confidence!

What is your choice?...
Faith or Fear?
Action or Regrets?

"It's not the events of our lives that shape us but our beliefs as to what those events mean."

- Anthony Robbins

DAY 9

Empowering Questions?

What fear did you face today?

_____

_____

_____

_____

What were your answers to the two EMPOWERING questions?
- *What's the worst thing that can happen if I take action?*
- *If I don't take action, what will it cost me?*

_____

_____

_____

_____

What action did you take?

_____

_____

_____

_____

What results did your actions produce?

_____

_____

_____

_____

"I've got my faith, and that's all I need."

- Nelson Mandela

DAY 10

Empowering Questions

What fear did you face today?

_____

_____

_____

_____

What were your answers to the two EMPOWERING questions?

- *What's the worst thing that can happen if I take action?*
- *If I don't take action, what will it cost me?*

_____

_____

_____

_____

What action did you take?

_____

_____

_____

_____

What results did your actions produce?

_____

_____

_____

_____

"No life will ever be great until it is dedicated and disciplined."

- Peter C. B. Bynoe

DAY 11

Empowering Questions

What fear did you face today?

_____
_____
_____
_____

What were your answers to the two EMPOWERING questions?
- *What's the worst thing that can happen if I take action?*
- *If I don't take action, what will it cost me?*

_____
_____
_____
_____

What action did you take?

_____
_____
_____
_____

What results did your actions produce?

_____
_____
_____
_____

"You're on earth for a purpose. Everyone's goal should be to find that purpose and to walk on the path to your destiny."

- Damon Wayans

Discovering What You Really Want

There is GREATNESS within you.

No matter what happened yesterday, remember: TODAY is a new day! In order to live your desired lifestyle, you must make the most of today. Think about it like this:

The past is gone. You can't change it. To be honest, the past is history. And the future is always out there: tomorrow, next week, next year…Therefore, the future is a mystery. So when it's all said and done, all you really have is the here and now.

And that is why we call it "PRESENT"…

because it is a gift.

The Clock ...keeps on ticking.

Putting first things first is the key to a fulfilling life. Think about it—five years from now, you will be five years older. You can't get around this. Time waits for no one.

The clock keeps on ticking.

So the question is: "When you reflect upon your life, will you be happy with your accomplishments or will you be sad because you have so many regrets?"

Now is the time to take action to ensure your future happiness.

Realize this: You are where you are today because of what you did yesterday. And where you will be tomorrow is determined by what you do today. It's that simple.

Do you understand that you were born on purpose?

You have so much potential. Think about it. There is no one on Earth who is exactly like you.

Even if you are an identical twin, you are still unique in certain aspects.

That's right, you are truly one of a kind.

In a few moments, you will stop reading and go look at yourself in the mirror for one full minute - 60 seconds. Yes, I'm serious. After you read this page, get up and look at yourself in the mirror. Take your time and really look at yourself.

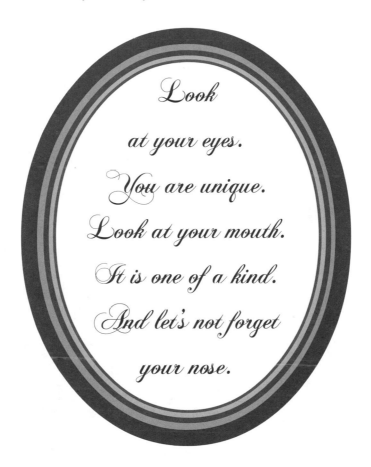

Look

at your eyes.

You are unique.

Look at your mouth.

It is one of a kind.

And let's not forget

your nose.

That's right, look at it. Don't try to hide from the truth. It is YOUR nose!

I could go on and on, but you get the point. You are truly unique. For a full 60 seconds, I'm asking you to look at yourself in the mirror. Take your time and really look at yourself.

OK, let's begin.

Stop reading and go look at yourself in the mirror for 60 seconds.

What did you see when you looked at yourself?

_____

_____

_____

_____

_____

_____

_____

_____

_____

_____

_____

_____

For some people, looking in the mirror for a full 60 seconds without any distractions (like brushing your teeth or combing your hair) is a new experience.

> ## "Most people search high and wide for the key to success. If they only knew that the key to their dreams lies within."
> *- George Washington Carver*

So why were you born with your unique characteristics? Why were you born into your particular family? Why do you live where you live?

> *There is a reason for why you are who you are. And the reason is: You were born for a specific purpose. Things do not happen by luck or chance. Your unique characteristics and your previous experiences have contributed to who you are today.*

Have you ever asked, "What is my life really all about?"

Imagine if someone came to you and said, ***"I am here to make three wishes come true for you!"***

What would your three wishes be?

And you cannot say,

"One of my wishes is for MORE wishes."

Think about it. ***"What are your three wishes?"***

What will you say?

My FIRST wish is:

_____
_____
_____
_____
_____

My SECOND wish is:

_____
_____
_____
_____
_____

My THIRD wish is:

_____
_____
_____
_____
_____

Now review each wish and write your reasons for why you made that particular wish.

Congratulations on reflecting upon your three wishes *and the reasons why they are important to you. Your three wishes tell a lot about what you value.*

Now here's a big question: Have you taken any action to make these three wishes come true?

Be honest.

List the specific actions that you have taken this year.

_____

_____

_____

_____

_____

_____

_____

_____

_____

_____

_____

_____

_____

_____

_____

_____

_____

_____

_____

_____

_____

_____

_____

_____

_____

If you have done specific things, I say, "CONGRATULATIONS!" because you are taking charge of your life by being on purpose.

If you say, "Nothing!" then it's now time to make your dreams a priority. Your assignment is to take action on making your wishes a reality.

You may be thinking, "Come on, Marlon, there's no way I can make these wishes come true."

My only response to you is, "It's possible!" Think about it...

For Dr. Martin Luther King to stand up to a racist Jim Crow segregation system with police dogs and church bombings illustrates the power of believing, *"It's possible!"*

For Nelson Mandela to spend 27 years of his life in prison because he believed in equal rights for all people and to then become president during the first democratic election in South Africa illustrates the power of believing, *"It's possible!"*

So don't tell me it can't be done because: **C + B = A**

When you **C**onceive a dream and **B**elieve with all your heart that *it's possible,* you can **A**chieve it.

Go for it!
Believe it's possible.
Take action now.

Remember, nothing happens unless you take action. Your assignment for the next two days is to take action to make your wishes a reality.

"People ask me how I built my business. I tell them that I didn't have much, but I used everything I had."

- Thomas Burrell

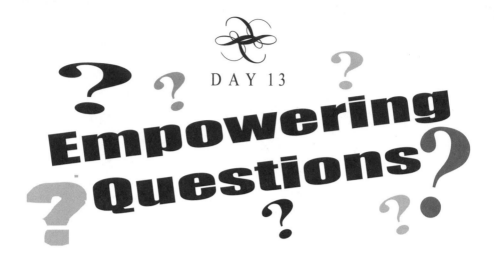

DAY 13

Empowering Questions

What did you do today to move closer to making Wish #1 a reality?

_____
_____
_____
_____

What did you do today to move closer to making Wish #2 a reality?

_____
_____
_____
_____

What did you do today to move closer to making Wish #3 a reality?

_____
_____
_____
_____

How do you now feel because you have taken action?

_____
_____
_____
_____

"I did it through persistence, dedication and hard work. You've got to find something you can apply your heart and soul to. People will say, 'No way'...but as long as you're persistent and determined, no one can stop you."

- Matty Rich

DAY 14

Empowering Questions

What did you do today to move closer to making Wish #1 a reality?

_____

_____

_____

_____

What did you do today to move closer to making Wish #2 a reality?

_____

_____

_____

_____

What did you do today to move closer to making Wish #3 a reality?

_____

_____

_____

_____

How do you now feel because you have taken action?

_____

_____

_____

_____

"The difference between what we do and what we are capable of doing would suffice to solve most of the world's problems."

- Mahatma Ghandi

DAY 15

Getting Clear On Your Goals

"Where there is no vision, the people perish!"

Is this really true?

Absolutely!

Right now, many people are physically alive, walking around, but they are emotionally dead.

What exactly do I mean?

These people are just sleep-walking, caught up in the same routine of doing the same things over and over. They have no passion because they are not clear on their purpose in life.

And it does not have to be like this.

Once you obtain more clarity regarding your vision, goals, and mission, your life takes on new meaning. You will have more energy and excitement because your life now has purpose.

It's what makes life worth living!

We all have something inside us that makes us want to do, see, and accomplish more. It gets us up early and keeps us up late at night. Goals are very important because they inspire us to be better.

Your goals fulfill you, give you hope, and add purpose to your life.

Some people ask, "If goals are so important, then what stops people from making their goals a priority?" Perhaps they're discouraged, unmotivated, or scared of failing. Or maybe they're listening to others who say, "It can't be done."

When you are committed to doing something positive with your life, it does not matter what other people say about your vision or your goals. If you have a vision that excites you and makes a positive difference, go for it with all your heart!

Because if you don't give 100% to achieving your goals, you'll be frustrated. You'll know in your heart that you could have done more. You'll have regrets because life has passed you by so quickly. You'll always wonder, "What would have happened if I had taken action?" Knowing there is something that speaks to your heart and not acting on your purpose will make you feel dead inside.

That's it! No more sleep-walking.

No more "Would of... Could of... Should of... BUT Didn't!"

Do you know where the richest place is on our planet?

No, it's not the banks!

No, it's not the gold mines or diamond mines!

No, it's not the home of a billionaire!

The richest place on Earth is the cemetery.

That's right, you heard me correctly.

The cemetery is the RICHEST place on Earth because so many people have died with their vision and goals still in them.

They never made their vision and goals a priority.

They just continued to say, "Tomorrow, I'll start," but that never happened.

And then they died with all their potential still in them.

How sad. It didn't have to end up like this.

Are you going to die with your most important goal still in you?

You deserve better than that!

Your vision needs to be nurtured and encouraged. Hold onto your goals and make them happen. Imagine how it will feel knowing that what was once a dream is now a reality.

> *"Excellence is to do a common thing in an uncommon way."*
>
> *- Booker T. Washington*

It may take some time to clearly determine your most important goals, and that's okay. Make the time to reflect upon your true purpose. Achieving your goals may not happen immediately. Don't worry. Just break your goals into specific steps—the journey of 100 miles always begins with the first step. And definitely celebrate your daily victories because you are taking action and making your dreams come true.

Keep believing in yourself because anything worth having is worth the effort.

Assignment

Goal Setting

Step #1:

Where are you going?

Brainstorm a list of anything you want to achieve, create, give, have, do, and/or experience in the next 20 years.

_____

_____

_____

_____

_____

_____

_____

_____

_____

_____

_____

_____

_____

_____

_____

_____

_____

_____

Step #2:

What is your timeframe?

Go back through your list and write 1, 3, 5, 10, or 20 years next to each goal to indicate how long it will take you to achieve each goal.

Step #3:

What are your TOP one-year goals?
Review your list again and write your four, most-important, one-year goals. Write down **why** you are absolutely committed to achieving each goal within the next twelve months.

GOAL #1:

_____

_____

Why?

_____

_____

GOAL #2:

_____

_____

Why?

_____

_____

GOAL #3:

_____

_____

Why?

_____

_____

GOAL #4:

_____

_____

Why?

_____

_____

Step #4:

Who will you become in the process of achieving your goals?
Write down what kind of person it will take to achieve all that you want. Describe the character traits, values, beliefs, and virtues that you will embody as you achieve your goals.

"Living in Hollywood can give you a false sense of reality. I try to stay in touch with my inner feelings — that's what's really going on."

- Will Smith

DAY 16

Empowering Questions

Who will be your mentor(s) in helping you achieve your goals?

_____
_____
_____
_____
_____

What other resources are available that will help you be successful?

_____
_____
_____
_____
_____

What books can you read and what classes can you take to help you achieve your goals?

_____
_____
_____
_____
_____

"Success always leaves footprints."

- Booker T. Washington

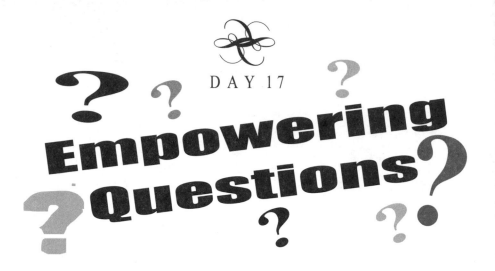

DAY 17
Empowering Questions

What did you do today to move closer to achieving your goals?

_____
_____
_____
_____
_____
_____

How does it feel to take action?

_____
_____
_____
_____
_____
_____

What can you do better or more efficiently to achieve your goals?

_____
_____
_____
_____
_____
_____

"The secret to success is to learn to accept the impossible, to do without the indispensable, and to bear the intolerable."

- Nelson Mandela

Empowering Questions

What have you learned as a result of striving for your goals?

_____

_____

_____

_____

_____

_____

_____

What areas do you need to improve in order to achieve your goals?

_____

_____

_____

_____

_____

_____

_____

How can you inspire others to focus on their goals and take action?

_____

_____

_____

_____

_____

_____

"Goals are the starting point to your future."

- M.C. Smith

Congratulations

On Gaining More Clarity On Your Goals

You are now in an elite group of leaders who are taking action rather than making excuses.

I applaud you because you are not settling for just being average. Rather, you are demanding more from yourself so that you may experience all of life.

As an additional tool for encouragement and inspiration, you are now going to create your *Goals Affirmation Collage*.

This collage will inspire you to keep going when you get tired or even when you want to give up!

I am not sharing this *Goals Affirmation Collage* from theory or something I read in a book. Rather, I am sharing the power of this *Goals Affirmation Collage* from my real-life experiences.

For the past number of years, I have been creating *Goals Affirmation Collages* to energize my purpose and focus. Every time I create a new collage, I am inspired to step up and make the most of every day because I'm reconnecting with my passion and purpose.

You will experience more passion and focus as you develop your *Goals Affirmation Collages.*

Let's make it happen!

Steps for Creating Your Goals Affirmation Collage

1. If possible, play some inspirational music.

2. Obtain old magazines and cut out pictures that bring a smile to your face. You can also collect photographs of special occasions that bring back fond memories of when you were truly blessed.

3. Paste or tape these pictures onto a large poster board.

4. Cut out positive quotes (that mean something to you) from various magazines and glue them onto your collage.

5. Write your own quotes on your collage with different colored magic markers.

6. Feel free to make as many collages as you desire.

7. Post your *Goals Affirmation Collages* on your bedroom walls, on your refrigerator, in your bathroom and any other places that you see regularly.

8. Slide a smaller collage (8.5" by 11" dimensions) into a plastic cover (so it is not damaged) and put it into a binder that you take with you wherever you go.

9. Review your *Goals Affirmation Collages* at least three times a day (morning, afternoon, and evening).

"It's not what you take but what you leave behind that defines greatness."

- Edward Gardner

DAY 20

Empowering Questions

What is your *Goals Affirmation Collage* doing for you?

_____
_____
_____
_____

How do you feel when you review your *Goals Affirmation Collage?*

_____
_____
_____
_____

How has your life taken on new meaning as a result of reviewing your *Goals Affirmation Collage?*

_____
_____
_____
_____

When you're feeling tired or frustrated, how does your *Goals Affirmation Collage* inspire you?

_____
_____
_____
_____

"It is better to be prepared for an opportunity and not have one, than to have an opportunity and not be prepared."

- Whitney Young

DAY 21

Empowering Questions

What are your strengths?

_____
_____
_____
_____
_____
_____

What are ten action items that you will do to achieve your goals?

_____
_____
_____
_____
_____
_____

When challenges come up, what will you do to still take action and move forward?

_____
_____
_____
_____
_____
_____
_____

"It is not your environment, it is you —
the quality of your mind, the integrity of
your soul and the determination of your
will that decides your future and shapes
your life."

- Benjamin E. Mays

DAY 22

Claiming the Power of Your Thoughts

So if it's true that each of us is born on purpose, you may be asking, "Why don't I feel successful and happy all the time?"

That's a great question. And the answer is: "What you focus on becomes your reality."

Whether you're happy or sad, it is determined by your perspective. **What you focus on in life is what you get in life!**

Think about it. Right now, at this very moment, what are some specific things that make you happy? Write your answers here:

_____
_____
_____
_____
_____

And on the other side, what things could you focus on right now to make you feel sad?

_____
_____
_____
_____
_____

So how is it that you can immediately change how you feel, from being happy to sad, in a few seconds?

Think about it! It all comes down to what you focus on. That's what determines how you feel.

Regardless of what happens to you, what's most important is how you perceive the situation to be.

When I'm experiencing a challenge or negativity, I always ask myself two empowering questions:
1) What can I learn from this situation?
2) How can I successfully resolve this challenge?

Our beliefs determine our happiness.

My personal belief is:

"Everything that happens in my life happens for a reason and it's ultimately for my benefit."

With this empowering belief, I am able to focus my thoughts on the positive outcome in any situation.

Is it easy? No, but it can be done. It just takes commitment.

Are you up for the challenge? I believe you are because you want the best out of life.

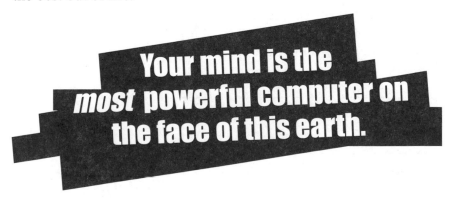

Your mind is the *most* powerful computer on the face of this earth.

Do you understand what this means?

Your mind is more powerful than any computer you see.

Let this statement soak in. Comprehend its true meaning. Your mind is power! And that's why you must master your thoughts— what you focus on is what you get.

When dealing with any situation, it is your thoughts that determine whether you feel positive emotions or negative emotions. You are in control of your thoughts. Therefore, you ultimately control how you feel. It's that simple.

I once asked a friend, "Are you happy?"

He looked me straight in the eyes, smiled and replied, "Marlon, I'm definitely happy because any day above ground is a great day. I'm alive and that means I still have more to do with my life."

This is an AWESOME perspective to have because you now appreciate what you have rather than focusing on what you don't have.

So what is your perspective towards life?

You may be thinking, "Okay, Marlon, so you want me to be happy-go-lucky, smiling like everything is great. That is just not realistic."

Well, let me ask you a question, "What is reality?"
What is your definition of the word: REALITY? Write your definition.

_____
_____
_____
_____
_____

To me, in simple terms, "Your perception is YOUR reality!"

This explains why two people can experience the exact same situation, yet have two different perspectives. One person feels great about the situation while the other person feels terrible.

A story of two men working for a construction company illustrates this point.

Two men, Chris and Jim, have the exact same job of laying bricks for a construction company. During the summer, a high school student is hired at the construction site. Walking from the office, the student sees Jim laying bricks. Being excited to have a job, the student walks over to Jim and says, "This is my first day on the job and I'm excited to be here. So how do you like your job?" Jim stops, frowns and replies with anger, "I hate it. I'm just laying bricks." Shocked, the high school student walks away confused.

A few hours later, the student meets Chris in another area of the construction site. He is also laying bricks. The student notices that Chris is smiling and singing while laying bricks. The student approaches Chris and asks the same question, "How do you like your job?" Chris smiles and responds, "I love it! I'm laying the foundation for my future."

Years later, the boy returns to the construction company and sees Jim, the first man whom he met while he was still in high school. Jim is doing the exact same thing that he was doing years earlier—laying bricks. The boy approaches Jim and initiates a conversation. The boy does not see Chris so he asks, "Where is your friend who was also laying bricks years ago?"

Jim stops and says, "Oh, you're talking about Chris. Well, he's been promoted. In fact, he's gone from one promotion to another. And today, he's the marketing vice president for this construction company." Jim stops abruptly and just stares at the brick he's holding in his hand.

The boy walks off thinking to himself, "Wow, both men had the exact same job a few years ago. And now, years later, one man is in the same job while his friend has been promoted to marketing vice president. One man had a negative attitude and the other had a positive attitude and look at where they are today."

So who are you most like in your thinking—Jim with negative thoughts, or Chris with positive thoughts? This is a very profound question because your thoughts determine your reality.

Trust me, it is more beneficial for you to focus your thoughts on things that are going "right" rather than things that are going "wrong."

It's Your Perspective!
It's Your Life!

??? Empowering Questions ?

What are your best characteristics?

_____
_____
_____
_____
_____

What are some of your proudest moments?

_____
_____
_____
_____
_____

When were the last times you had BIG fun? What did you do?

_____
_____
_____
_____
_____
_____

Right now, what are you grateful to have in your life?

_____
_____
_____
_____
_____

So how do you feel now?

I'm sure you're feeling more positive because you have answered some

?Empowering? Questions?

The questions that we ask ourselves are critically important because they direct our attention. Remember, whatever question you ask of yourself, you will get an answer.

Our self-talk ultimately determines whether we are happy or sad.

Have you ever watched little kids on a playground?

There they are playing, creating their own fun.

They're laughing, joking and smiling.

Think back to when you were younger. It was the little things that made you smile.

Maybe it was after a big rainstorm and you went jumping from one puddle of water to another. Or it could have been how you lost time as you laid on your back, looking up to the sky, making pictures out of the clouds. Or maybe it was playing fun games with your friends.

> *Those were the days, huh?*
>
> *Life was so care free and fun!*
>
> *Time flew by so quickly because*
>
> *you were having so much fun!*

Regardless of how old you are, it's now time to have more fun. That's right! It's now time to have MORE FUN in your life.

Now hear me straight! I'm not saying you have to go jumping in some puddles of water to have fun.

But I'm sure there are other things you can do to experience incredible joy and excitement.

So let's go for it. Your assignment is for the next six days to do something totally fun as you learn NEW information. Have Fun!

If you are thinking, "This is stupid. I'm older now, no longer a child," then this is my question to you: "Who said you can't still have fun?"

Listen up!

Tomorrow is not promised, so why not enjoy today to the fullest? Give yourself the gift of **at least one fun activity while learning NEW information every day** for the next six days.

If you still need some encouragement to take action, ponder this thought:

You're at the doctor's office. You have just taken your medical examination. The blood tests are complete. The doctor walks back into your room and says, "I'm sorry but you only have ONE month to live."

We don't need to be motivated to take action because of a negative medical report. Instead, get motivated because you deserve to enjoy your life. Let's begin. Day One is now!

What is your fun activity for today? As a student, what will you do to enjoy the process of learning new information? Remember, obtaining an education can be fun. You just have to be creative.

Don't be one of those people who just looks at life as a hard struggle and forgets how to have fun.

☺ *Smiling is good for your heart.*

Have Fun TODAY!

Laughing is good for your soul.

Having fun is exhilarating because it's good for your mind, body and spirit. Enjoy life because you deserve it! Have Fun Today!

"I had heard all kinds of rumors about MIT. They used to say that even the janitors at MIT had Master's degrees. At first I wasn't going, but then I couldn't run away from a challenge. I had to compete with the best." - Ronald McNair

Assignment

 For the next six days, you will do at least one thing that makes you enjoy school more. Smile, laugh and have fun while you learn NEW information. I'm talking about stepping outside your comfort zone and having fun.

The only guidelines are that these activities must be clean fun and good for you and everyone else.

After completing your fun activity, you will record the activity and write how you felt while experiencing the activity.

For example, maybe you'll talk to some of your classmates and form a study group where you do your homework together. Or maybe you'll go see your teachers after school for some extra help, or maybe you'll watch a documentary movie that deals with what you are learning in your history class. It's up to you. Be creative.

Remember, you were born on purpose and your education will help you achieve your goals. Learning can also take place outside a formal education. Be creative!

"In one hand I have an idea, in the other, I have an obstacle. Which one grabs your attention?"

- Henry Parker

D A Y 23

What did you do today to have more fun while learning NEW information?

_____
_____
_____
_____
_____
_____
_____
_____

How did you feel?

_____
_____
_____
_____
_____
_____
_____
_____
_____

What did you enjoy the most?

_____
_____
_____
_____
_____
_____
_____
_____
_____

"Remember, luck is opportunity meeting up with preparation, so you must prepare yourself to be lucky."

- *Gregory Hines*

D A Y 24

What did you do today to have more fun while learning NEW information?

_____
_____
_____
_____
_____
_____
_____
_____
_____

How did you feel?

_____
_____
_____
_____
_____
_____
_____
_____
_____

What did you enjoy the most?

_____
_____
_____
_____
_____
_____
_____
_____
_____

"I figured that if I said it enough, I would convince the world that I really was the greatest."

- Muhammad Ali

DAY 25

What did you do today to have more fun while learning NEW information?

_____
_____
_____
_____
_____
_____
_____
_____

How did you feel?

_____
_____
_____
_____
_____
_____
_____
_____

What did you enjoy the most?

_____
_____
_____
_____
_____
_____
_____
_____

"The only place where success comes before work is in the dictionary."

- S.B. Fuller

DAY 26

What did you do today to have more fun while learning NEW information?

_____
_____
_____
_____
_____
_____
_____
_____

How did you feel?

_____
_____
_____
_____
_____
_____
_____
_____

What did you enjoy the most?

_____
_____
_____
_____
_____
_____
_____
_____

"Either move or be moved!"

- Colin Powell

D A Y 27

What did you do today to have more fun while learning NEW information?

_____

_____

_____

_____

_____

_____

_____

_____

How did you feel?

_____

_____

_____

_____

_____

_____

_____

_____

What did you enjoy the most?

_____

_____

_____

_____

_____

_____

_____

_____

"A person completely wrapped up in himself makes a small package."

- Denzel Washington

DAY 28

What did you do today to have more fun while learning ▮NEW▮ **information?**

_____
_____
_____
_____
_____
_____
_____
_____
_____

How did you feel?

_____
_____
_____
_____
_____
_____
_____
_____
_____

What did you enjoy the most?

_____
_____
_____
_____
_____
_____
_____
_____
_____

"Some men see things as they are and ask why. Others dream things that never were and ask why not."

- George Bernard Shaw

Living Your True Mission

Have you ever noticed how time seems to fly by so quickly?

Right now, for the next sixty seconds, look at your watch.

Get ready, get set, GO!

Tick... Tock... Tick... Tock... Tick... Tock... Sixty seconds!

So what makes the difference between why some people achieve great things and others are just barely making it?

Think about it. We all have the same 24 hours in a day, and yet different results are produced by different people.

Why do you think this is?

_____
_____
_____
_____
_____
_____
_____
_____
_____
_____
_____

Did you include the word "Priorities" in your answer?

The ultimate difference between achieving your goals and having regrets is determined by whether or not you are:

1) **Absolutely clear and focused on your goals / priorities, and**

2) **Taking consistent action daily to achieve your goals.**

It's unfortunate that some people feel like they are on a never-ending treadmill. They are taking action but feel like they are going nowhere.

So how do you get off the treadmill?

That's the $1 million question. And the answer is... "Get clear on your true priorities, stay focused, and take action."

Sounds simple, huh? Yes, it is simple! But for some people, it's not easy.

Understand this, I'm talking about living a truly fulfilling life. I am not talking about just being focused on your priorities for a week or a month or even for the rest of this year. Rather, I'm talking about putting first things first, taking action, and staying focused on your goals and priorities EVERY day.

You may be thinking, "Sounds great! But how do I do it?"

To help you be your best and live an awesome life, you will now develop your personal **mission statement.**

Writing a mission statement is a tremendous opportunity for self-discovery. Living with a mission statement makes life more meaningful and exciting. **The purpose of creating a mission statement is to have something to use as a guide and to keep focused on what's really important to you.** It imprints your values and dreams firmly in your mind so you may be, speak and live as your ideal self.

Once you have developed your mission statement, I suggest that you refer to it daily in order to keep your vision consistently before you. Periodically, review and evaluate your mission statement to keep in touch with your own development and to keep in harmony with your deepest self. Then, update your mission statement when necessary because as your life changes, your mission statement will also expand.

To help you create a powerful life mission statement, answer the following six questions:

1. At your funeral, what do you want people to say about you?

_____
_____
_____
_____
_____
_____
_____
_____

2. For you to be your best, what do you have to do everyday?

_____
_____
_____
_____
_____
_____

3. What do you value most in your life?

_____
_____
_____
_____
_____
_____

4. What do you have to remember in order to feel great about who you are right now?

_____

_____

_____

_____

_____

_____

_____

_____

5. How do you prioritize your values (love, fun, happiness, security, growth, peace, power, contribution and etc.)? Rank your top-10 values.

_____

_____

_____

_____

_____

_____

_____

_____

_____

_____

6. What exactly do you want to accomplish with your life?

_____

_____

_____

_____

_____

_____

_____

Any breakthroughs? I'm sure there were. This is a powerful first step. Now let's create your mission statement. To help you develop your mission statement, I will share *my mission statement* as an example.

I, Marlon Christopher Smith, see, hear, feel and know that the purpose of my life is to be a shining, smiling light, enjoying the daily miracles, doing fun and exciting things with others and for myself, growing where I am better then the previous day, co-creating with God as I maximize my true potential while helping make the world a better place.

Now it's your turn! Go ahead and be creative.

I, _____, see, hear, feel and know that the purpose of my life is to:

_____

_____

_____

_____

_____

_____

_____

Congratulations!

You now have your personal mission statement. Feel free to revisit your mission statement and add to it. In life, you will continue to grow and change. Thus, your mission statement will also expand and evolve over time.

"The way to be successful is through preparation. It doesn't just happen. You don't wake up one day and discover you're a lawyer any more than you wake up as a pro football player. It takes time."

- Alan Page

Today's assignment is to complete your

Mission Statement Board

To make your mission statement come alive, get some magic markers and poster boards. Write your mission statement on your poster boards and put them up throughout your home (on your bedroom walls, on the refrigerator, and on the bathroom mirror), at school (in your locker and in your school binder) and/or at your job (on your desk and in your time management planner).

Every time you see your mission statement, read it aloud with energy and excitement. You may even add some pictures and motivational quotes to your mission statement boards. This will definitely spice up your energy when you look at your mission statement.

Empowering Questions

Since writing your mission statement, how do you now view life? By understanding your mission, do you have new ideas and thoughts?

_____

_____

_____

_____

_____

_____

"If there is no struggle, there is no progress."

- Frederick Douglass

D A Y 3 1

Congratulations

On creating your *Mission Statement Board*

Now let's really engrain your mission statement within your mind and your heart.

In the morning before you get out of bed, and in the evening before you go to bed, recite your mission statement with passion and energy. Memorize your mission statement and recite it throughout the day.

What does your mission statement mean to you?

_____
_____
_____
_____
_____
_____
_____
_____
_____
_____

"The tragedy of life doesn't lie in not reaching your goal. The tragedy lies in having no goal to reach."

- Benjamin E. Mays

Assignment

Ask your family and friends to share their mission statements with you. If they do not have one, go ahead and share how your personal mission statement has impacted your life. Share the steps so they may also develop their personal mission statements.

Whom did you ask regarding their personal mission statements and what were their responses?

_____
_____
_____
_____
_____

Of those you asked, how many had a life mission statement?

_____
_____
_____
_____
_____

Who did you help in developing his/her mission statement?

_____
_____
_____
_____
_____

How does it feel to help others develop their mission statements?

_____
_____
_____
_____
_____
_____
_____
_____
_____
_____
_____
_____
_____
_____
_____
_____
_____
_____

What did you learn by having conversations with others about the importance of having a mission statement?

_____
_____
_____
_____
_____
_____
_____
_____
_____
_____
_____
_____
_____
_____
_____
_____

"When you face a crisis, you know who your true friends are."

- Earvin "Magic" Johnson

Empowering Questions

How are you going to make a difference in the world?

_____
_____
_____
_____
_____
_____
_____
_____
_____
_____

When you are 95 years old and look back on your life, what will make you smile?

_____
_____
_____
_____
_____
_____
_____
_____
_____
_____
_____
_____

"Always strive to be more than that which you are, if you wish to obtain that which you are not."

- S.B. Fuller

DAY 34

Empowering Questions

What will it take to accomplish your mission?

_____
_____
_____
_____
_____
_____
_____
_____
_____
_____

What will you do by the end of this year?

_____
_____
_____
_____
_____
_____
_____
_____
_____
_____

"The key to my success has been to give up everything for my dream."

- John H. Johnson

DAY 35

Empowering Questions

When things get challenging, how will you stay motivated to continue taking action?

_____

_____

_____

_____

_____

_____

_____

_____

_____

_____

What are you doing to make the best use of your time?

_____

_____

_____

_____

_____

_____

_____

_____

_____

_____

"Time is the most precious commodity because once gone, it can never be recaptured."

- M.C. Smith

Enjoying a Balanced Life

The six primary areas of your life are:

1. School / Work
2. Physical Health
3. Emotions
4. Finances
5. Relationships
6. Spiritual

What would you rather have:

HEALTH

OR

WEALTH?

Explain your answer:

_____
_____
_____
_____
_____
_____
_____
_____
_____
_____
_____
_____
_____
_____

Many people say, "Wealth," not realizing that without your health, it does not matter how much money you have because you will not be able to fully enjoy it.

For you to have an extraordinary life, you must have balance. If any particular area of your life is out of balance, it will impact the other areas of your life.

Today, you will take an honest look at your life. Review the *Wheel of Life* on this page.

The center of the wheel represents 0% (terrible results) and the circumference represents 100% (fantastic results), indicating where you ideally want to be in each area of your life.

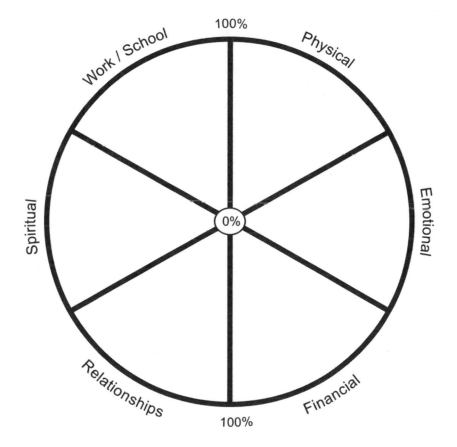

You will give yourself a percentage (%) which represents where you currently are in each of the six areas of your life.

As an example, look at how John evaluates his life.

Category	%	Reasons Why John Gave His Particular Scores
School / Work	50%	Because he is doing okay in school but knows he can do much better if he will study more and participate in group sessions with his classmates.
Physical	90%	Because he is first-string on the basketball team and only needs to improve his 3-point shooting.
Emotional	40%	Because he pretends to be happy but he has some major insecurities that need to be addressed.
Financial	20%	Because he has a part-time job but he just spends and spends. He needs to develop a budget and save some money for his future goals.
Relationships	60%	Because he is close to his mom and sister and has honest conversations with them. However, he wants his relationship with his father to improve.
Spiritual	80%	Because he prays everyday and feels centered.

Here's John's Wheel of Life:

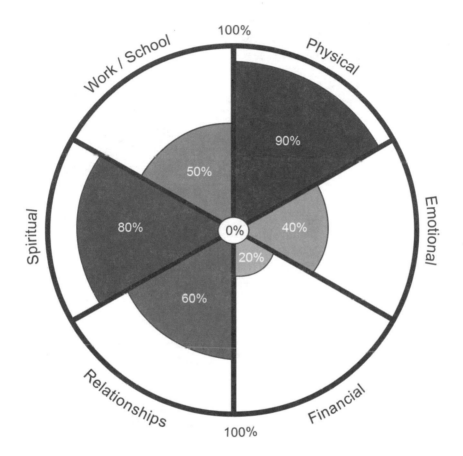

Now it's your turn. Remember, this is just a snapshot of where you feel you are today. There are no judgments, so just be honest with yourself.

Category	%	The Reasons Why I Gave My Particular Score
School / Work		
Physical		
Emotional		
Financial		
Relationships		
Spiritual		

On the following *Wheel of Life*, draw a line representing the percentage (%) that you currently feel you are in each of the six areas. Once you have drawn your lines, shade in each particular area of the wheel.

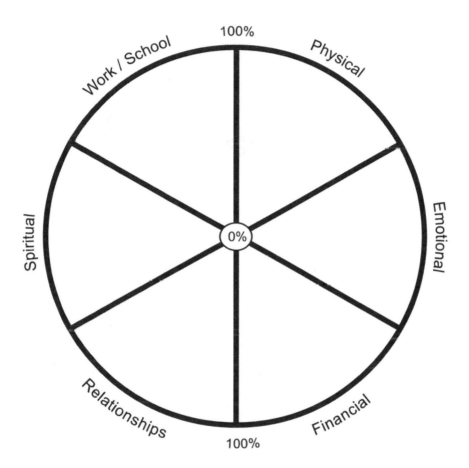

What did you learn from completing this exercise?

_____
_____
_____
_____
_____
_____
_____
_____
_____
_____

If your _Wheel of Life_ is a wheel on a car called "life," how will the car run? What if you are going 20 miles per hour?

_____
_____
_____
_____
_____
_____
_____
_____
_____
_____

And what if you are a high achiever with more responsibilities and a busier life? How will life feel if your car is now going 100 miles per hour?

_____
_____
_____
_____
_____
_____
_____
_____
_____

Review your Wheel of Life

It is expected that some areas will be stronger than others indicating that they need more attention.

Creating more balance in your life will make a difference. If any particular area of your life is out of balance, it will definitely impact your other areas.

Putting more time, energy and focus into all six areas will allow you to have an EXTRAORDINARY life.

 Your assignment is to do specific things for the next three days that will create more balance in your life.

"The collapse of character begins with compromise."

- Frederick Douglass

D A Y 37

Empowering Questions?

What did you do with your time today to create more balance in your life?

_____
_____
_____
_____
_____

What did you learn?

_____
_____
_____
_____
_____

How do you feel about your progress?

_____
_____
_____
_____
_____
_____

"If it's to be, it's up to me!"

DAY 38

Empowering Questions

What did you do with your time today to create more balance in your life?

_____
_____
_____
_____
_____

What did you learn?

_____
_____
_____
_____
_____
_____

How do you feel about your progress?

_____
_____
_____
_____
_____
_____

"The best preparation for tomorrow is to do your best today."

- Lou Gossett

DAY 39

Empowering Questions

What did you do with your time today to create more balance in your life?

_____

_____

_____

_____

_____

What did you learn?

_____

_____

_____

_____

_____

_____

How do you feel about your progress?

_____

_____

_____

_____

_____

_____

"The Seven P's: Prior Proper Planning Prevents Pitifully-Poor Performance."

D A Y 4 0

Based on the previous actions that you have taken, go ahead and complete the following *Wheel of Life* exercise, which indicates where you feel you are today.

Remember, this is just a snapshot of where you feel you are currently. There are no judgments, so just be honest with yourself. Let's begin.

Category	%	The Reasons Why I Gave My Particular Score
School / Work		
Physical		
Emotional		
Financial		
Relationships		
Spiritual		

On the following *Wheel of Life*, draw a line representing the percentage (%) that you currently feel you are in each of these six areas. Once you have drawn your lines, shade in each particular area of the wheel.

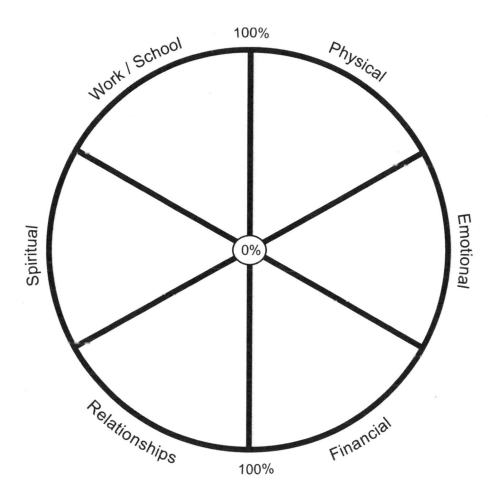

Now compare this *Wheel of Life* with the *Wheel of Life* that you previously completed on Day #36.

Do you notice some differences between your two wheels?

What are the major differences between your two *Wheels of Life?*

_____
_____
_____
_____
_____
_____
_____
_____
_____
_____

How important is it to have balance in your life?

_____
_____
_____
_____
_____
_____
_____
_____
_____
_____

What have you learned during these last few days?

_____
_____
_____
_____
_____
_____
_____
_____
_____
_____

"A winner never quits and a quitter never wins."

Congratulations!

You have stepped up and completed this 40-day

Living With Purpose program. You are definitely an

individual who has an exciting destiny. Do review your

answers and continue being your best because you deserve

all that life has to offer. Share your insights and

breakthroughs with your family and friends. Encourage

them to participate in this *Living With Purpose*

program or one of the other Success By Choice leadership

programs because they also deserve to maximize their true

potential. We are excited to hear from you. Share your

insights and breakthroughs with us by sending an email to:

purpose@successbychoice.com.

Stay Blessed,

Marlon

P.S. Remember, "Your Success is YOUR Choice!"

"Every new idea is an impossibility until it is born."

- Ron Brown

About the Author

A Young Man On A Mission

However, he has not always been blessed with this focus. As a young person, there were times when Marlon did not appreciate his true worth. He lacked confidence in his abilities, and to further complicate matters, he struggled in school. There was even a time when Marlon received a 1.6 GPA on his report card. No matter how much time he spent on his studies, some class material was just too "HARD" for him to comprehend. Many questioned his future.

But Marlon turned his life around! His confidence soared and his academic performance reached all new heights, where he obtained all "A's" a few semesters later.

Marlon graduated from the University of Virginia with a Bachelor of Science degree in Electrical Engineering. As a college student, Marlon's proudest moment came when he founded *Street Academics*, a high school outreach program. Each week, Marlon and his college friends went into local schools to share success strategies with younger students. Through his involvement, Marlon learned the power of "giving."

His corporate experience includes working at two Fortune-500 corporations, IBM and Hewlett-Packard in Silicon Valley. During his lunch breaks, Marlon went into various schools and shared inspirational insights with struggling students.

Ultimately, Marlon listened to his heart and resigned from Hewlett-Packard to follow his passion of helping young people make the right choices. And with faith, Success By Choice, Inc. was founded!

Marlon Smith

For the past 15 years, Marlon has been blessed with opportunities to inspire, entertain, and motivate thousands of individuals in 45 states, including Alaska

And because his message is so timely, he has traveled abroad on numerous speaking tours throughout the former Soviet Union (in Moscow, Gorney-Altay, Kazakhstan), Canada, Mexico, Japan, England, the Caribbean, Botswana, LeSotho, Ghana, Swaziland, and South Africa.

In South Africa, Marlon produced the *"Motivational Mondays"* television series as well as the national *"Success is Your Choice"* radio program, empowering the entire country.

In November 2004, Marlon was featured in ESSENCE Magazine as one of the top motivational speakers.

Marlon is the co-producer of the "REAL MEN TALKING" multimedia stage production, which is helping people throughout the United States maximize their true potential.

Marlon feels blessed to share his "Real-Life" experiences in helping others manifest their true greatness as they *live with purpose.*

ACKNOWLEDGEMENTS

I feel blessed to have so much support in my life. It is an honor and privilege to work with a team of extraordinary individuals.

Thelma Austin, CEO of Precise Communications/Praise Press (who is also my aunt), helped crystallize my thoughts by editing the book manuscript so **Living With Purpose** will effectively inspire people to take action. I appreciate your selflessness.

Malcolm Aaron, owner of Top Notch Designs, is the talented illustrator who has the ability to capture concepts with his pictures. I am grateful for your belief in me, your brother from another.

Myrna Urmanita, owner of Urmanita Designs, spent countless hours making sure every page was fun and exciting to read. I admire your commitment to excellence and your honest feedback.

Janelle Cipriano (Myrna's daughter), a student majoring in Advertising at the Academy of Art University in San Francisco, contributed her youthful energy and creativity in the design of the book. I am amazed at your professionalism and passion for giving your best.

Flemuel Brown, owner of Justice Productions, is the co-producer of Real Men Talking who contributed his input to completing the **Living With Purpose** DVD-based curriculum. I have enjoyed the journey of helping others maximize their true potential.

I have been blessed by all of your contributions. May God continue to direct your steps as you **Live With Purpose**!

CONTACT INFORMATION

Success By Choice, Inc. is an educational consulting firm specializing in motivational keynote presentations, leadership curriculum programs, on-line empowerment courses and "Edutainment" life-skills multimedia. For more information on Success By Choice, Inc., visit www.successbychoice.com.

To help inspire more people through the entertainment medium, one division of Success By Choice, Inc. has partnered with Justice Productions LLC to develop the **"Real Men Talking"** multimedia stage productions, music soundtracks, film and movie projects.

Traveling throughout the United States, different men were interviewed about what it means to be a "REAL" man. These interviews were edited into video clips for the **"Real Men Talking"** multimedia stage production and DVD-based curriculum. For more information on the **"Real Men Talking"** movement, visit www.realmentalking.com.

For more information, contact:
RMT International
1702 North 62nd Street Philadelphia, PA 19151
215-877-8172   FAX: 215-877-0788
showtime@realmentalking.com
www.realmentalking.com

"Real Men Talking Is A Must-See!"

Dr. Cornel West
Professor of Religion and African American Studies, Princeton University
*"This production is an affirmation of
the things I have been speaking on."*

The New Jersey Forum
*"A funny, informative, well-thought and presented play…
a performance most deserving of the red carpet."*

Solomon Jones
Entertainment Columnist, Philadelphia Weekly
"A phenomenal production for everybody."

Common
Hip Hop Artist (Geffen)
"I'm glad to be a part of something this positive."

Chuck D
Hip Hop Pioneer and Intellectual
"What these brothers are doing is what we need."

Dyanna Williams
Founder and President, International Association
of African American Musicians
"A brilliant performance and production."

Dr. Delores Saunders
National President, National Alliance of
Black School Educators (NABSE)
*"What a stellar performance.
It's just what our young boys and men need."*

Ozzie Jones
World-renowned Director and Creative Director,
Walt Whitman Arts Center, New Jersey
"An amazing performance by an amazing cast and director."

BIBLIOGRAPHY

Kimbro, Dennis. *Daily Motivations for African-American Success*. New York: The Random House Ballantine Publishing Group, 1993.

Warren, Rick. *The Purpose Driven Life*. Grand Rapids, MI: Zondervan, 2002.

Youth's Extraordinary Strategies for Peak Performance. San Diego, CA: Anthony Robbins Foundation, 2006.

Maxwell, John. *The Maxwell Leadership Bible (NKJV)*. Nashville, TN: Thomas Nelson Publishers, 1982.